spot

AWESOME NATURE

WEATHER

by K.C. Kelley

AMICUS

sun

clouds

Look for these words and pictures as you read.

lightning

tornado

Look at the blue sky!
The weather is warm today!

Earth has many
kinds of weather.
Sandstorms blow in deserts.
Rain soaks rain forests.

sun

Look at the sun.
The sun warms the air.
It helps plants grow.

clouds

Look at the clouds. Clouds can be white, gray, or black. They hold rain and snow.

lightning

See the lightning?
Lightning is a big spark.
A storm is coming!

See this tornado?
A tornado is a windstorm.
They spin fast.

tornado

There is a rainbow!
The storm is over!

sun

clouds

Did you find?

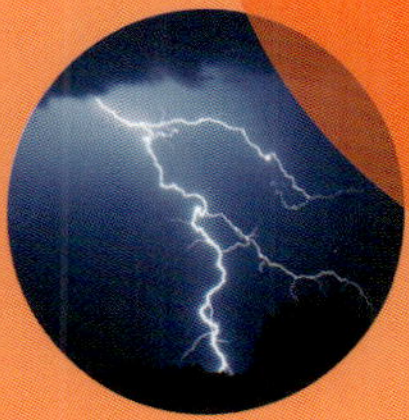

lightning

tornado

spot

Amicus Readers and Amicus Ink are imprints of Amicus
P.O. Box 1329, Mankato, MN 56002
www.amicuspublishing.us

Cataloging-in-Publication Data is on file with the Library of Congress
ISBN 978-1-68151-284-6 (library binding)
ISBN 978-1-68152-244-9 (paperback)
ISBN 978-1-68151-324-9 (eBook)

Printed in China

HC 10 9 8 7 6 5 4 3 2 1
PB 10 9 8 7 6 5 4 3 2 1

Megan Peterson, editor
Deb Miner, series designer
Patty Kelley, book designer
Producer/Photo Research:
Shoreline Publishing Group LLC

Photos:
Cover: Agnieszka Mac Uchman/Dreamstime.com. Inside: Dreamstime.com: Stephen Coburr 1, Jiajianzheng 2tl, Winzworks 2tr, Martin Fischer 2bl, Wisconsinart 2br, Serrnovik 3, Maksym Protsenko 6, Sanchik 8, Stnazkul 10, Justin Hobson 12, Shester171 14. Shutterstock: Lukasz Janyst 4.